quick &
sushi and sashimi

Susie Donald

Create delicious Japanese cuisine at home with dishes like Nigiri Sushi with Prawns, Tuna and Eel, Inside-out California Rolls and Inari Tofu Pouch Sushi.

PERIPLUS

Basic Kitchen Utensils

makisu

Bamboo rolling mat (*makisu*): Widely available from Japanese supermarkets and very inexpensive, this simple bamboo mat is a must-have utensil if you want to roll rice inside wrappers of seaweed, and for rolling Japanese omelets.

Chopsticks (*saibashi*): Look for the long wooden chopsticks used for cooking. Regular chopsticks are too short and may result in burns.

Fan (*uchiwa*): A useful implement for cooling cooked sushi rice but if you can't find one, make your own.

hangiri

Knife: Always use a very sharp knife and keep it out of reach of children. Regular kitchen knives are fine but do remember to avoid using a serrated knife when cutting fish to avoid tearing the flesh.

Wooden sushi rice bowl (*hangiri*): This low, wide wooden bowl is used to cool rice and give it the desired texture. The wider the bowl the better for you to separate the rice grains.

shamoji

Rice paddle (*shamoji*): This wooden scoop, which is used to spread cooked rice to cool in the *hangiri*, is perhaps the most symbolic kitchen utensil as it represents domestic authority. Whoever controls the *shamoji* in a Japanese household is surely in charge of the household affairs.

hone nuki

Fish-bone tweezers (*hone nuki*): A pair of flat-ended tweezers is always present in a Japanese kitchen for deboning fish.

Ingredients

Daikon is a large, white radish often eaten raw—sliced or grated into long, thin strips—with sashimi and tempura. It is also pickled and sold in jars. Available in most supermarkets, it is regarded as a healthy antidote for oily foods.

Dashi stock is the basic Japanese fish broth made from water, *konbu* (dried kelp) and bonito flakes (see recipe page 10). It is also available in an instant version in powdered or granule form. This is useful when a small amount of stock is required for sauces and as a seasoning.

Deep-fried tofu slices (*abura-age*) must be blanched before serving. When cut in half, these slices serve as delicious wrapping pouches (pages 26, 29).

Dried bonito flakes (*katsuo bushi*) are sold in plastic packs in the Japanese foods section of most supermarkets. The shavings come in varying sizes—larger flakes are used to make Basic Dashi Stock (page 10) whereas the finer ones are used as a garnish.

Fish sauce is a fermented fish seasoning made by layering fish and salt in large jars and then siphoning off the liquid. It is sold bottled and is a common seasoning in Thai and Vietnamese food.

Furikake is a dried seasoning mixture that is sprinkled over rice dishes and sushi. It consists of toasted seaweed, sesame seeds, ground dried fish and salt. Sold in small bottles in the Japanese food section of supermarkets.

Japanese cucumbers are smaller, thinner and sweeter than normal ones, and have much smaller seeds. Substitute baby cucumbers or pickling gherkins if unavailable.

Japanese mustard is similar to English mustard, but hotter—it is a blend of ground mustard seeds without any added flour. It can be purchased in powdered form in small cans or as a ready-to-use paste in tubes.

Kanpyo are long, thin strips of dried gourd that are used in making sushi and slow-cooked dishes; also for tying food together. They are sold in plastic packets in the dried foods section of Japanese stores, and many supermarkets.

Konbu is a dried kelp in the form of flat, black sheets with white powder on the surface, used to flavor Sushi Rice (pages 8-9) and Basic Dashi Stock (page 10). The kelp's flavor infuses quickly in water, so do not wash it before cooking—just wipe to remove any dust or powder. *Konbu* is often removed before a dish is served.

Lotus roots are tubers with a crunchy, starchy flavor in their raw form and a characteristic lacy pattern in cross-section. They are either sold covered in mud or cleaned and sealed in plastic packets.

Mirin is a sweet cooking wine made by mixing steamed glutinous rice with distilled spirits and sugar. The resulting liquid contains 12-14% alcohol. Avoid products labeled "*aji-mirin*" as they are a MSG-flavored version.

Miso is an important seasoning in Japan—a fermented paste made from soybeans and rice, wheat or barley. Available in various colors and flavors, but the most common are red and white misos, which are used in miso soups. Available in most supermarkets.

Nori are the dried leaves of a seaweed called laver, and are generally sold in 20 x 17 cm (8 x 7-in) sheets and used for wrapping sushi or cut into squares for cone sushi. *Nori* is best toasted before serving to make it crisp and fragrant (instructions on page 42). Also sold pretoasted and packed flat in bags.

Palm sugar varies in color from gold to dark brown and is made from the sap of the coconut or *arenga* palm. It has a rich flavor similar to dark brown sugar or maple syrup, both of which make good substitutes. Available in cylindrical cakes in plastic containers or packets.

Pickled Chinese olives are sold canned in brine. They are tapered at both ends and slightly elongated, and can be substituted with salted black Mediterranean olives.

Pickled Ginger are thin slices of young ginger that are pickled in salt, and then in vinegar. It is a popular accompaniment to sushi and sashimi. It is sold in jars and is widely available, but is also easy to make fresh (see recipe page 18).

Ponzu is a dressing made from citrus juice (lemon, lime or orange) mixed with soy, sugar and vinegar. Available bottled but you can also make your own fresh using the recipe on page 11.

Rice vinegar is a light, mildly tangy vinegar brewed from rice. Its color varies from almost white to pale gold.

Sake is a brewed Japanese rice wine. Chinese rice wine or dry sherry may be substituted.

Seasoned jellyfish is generally sold as salted or dried strips; it is commonly used in vinegared salads. It is sold in plastic packages in the refrigerator section of supermarkets.

Sesame oil should be used sparingly as a seasoning and never for frying. Japanese sesame oil is milder than the Chinese version, so when using the latter, dilute with a little vegetable oil.

Sesame paste is made from toasted sesame seeds that are ground up like peanut butter, but unsweetened. Available in most food stores, or make fresh by pan-roasting and then grinding the sesame seeds in a processor.

Shiso leaves (also known as perilla) have a fresh, slightly minty flavor. They are served with sashimi (and should be eaten with it), made into tempura and used in various ways to garnish sushi. Substitute mint leaves.

Short-grain Japanese rice can be readily purchased everywhere (see pages 8-9 for instructions on preparing Sushi Rice). Uncooked rice should be stored in an airtight container at room temperature.

Smoked conger eel (*anago*) is lightly boiled, then grilled and basted before serving. It may be purchased in packets in the refrigerator section of supermarkets.

Soy sauce (*shoyu*) is fermented from soy beans and salt, and commonly used in marinades, sauces and dips. Japanese soy sauce has a distinctive flavor and it is recommended that you purchase a bottle rather than use Chinese soy sauce for Japanese food.

Tezu vinegared water is a mixture of $1/2$ cup water and 1 tablespoon rice vinegar. It is used for moistening fingers when making sushi to prevent the rice from sticking to them.

Wakame is a type of seaweed available in dried strips which are light brown in color. It is often added to soups a few minutes before serving and has a crunchy texture. Soak in water for 5 to 10 minutes before using. Also sold seasoned and packed in plastic in the refrigerator section of the supermarket.

Wasabi (Japanese horseradish) is unrelated to Western horseradish but produces a similarly sharp, biting effect on the tongue and in the nose. It is used to season sushi and is commonly available in a powdered form or as a ready-made paste in plastic squeeze tubes.

Buying Fish for Sashimi and Sushi

The most important consideration when selecting fish to use for sushi and sashimi is freshness. Quite simply, if the fish and seafood used are not extremely fresh, then the sushi and sashimi will not be good.

For shellfish—both hard and soft-shelled—extremely fresh usually means alive at the time of purchase and kept alive until required.

The types of fish and seafood most commonly used in Japan are mentioned here, but these should only act as a guide. Most fish can be eaten raw so we recommend that you use whatever available fresh fish is in season.

As a rule, frozen fish should be avoided when preparing dishes to be eaten raw. This is not only due to the health risk associated with fish that is less than fresh, but also because the flavor and texture are usually compromised. A generally accepted exception to this rule is tuna and squid which have been flash-frozen. If your fishmonger can guarantee that the fish has been treated in this manner, then you will probably find it to be a satisfactory substitute.

Some fish and seafood are precooked before being used in sushi and sashimi, such as prawns, crab or lobster. Salmon is often smoked or salted; octopus and eel are often boiled or marinated. For sashimi, only the best parts or cuts are normally used. For example, the body of a squid (and not the tentacles) and only the prime fillets of a tuna are used.

Cutting Tips

Fish and seafood are usually cut into long, thin strips and pieces for sushi and sashimi. Use a long, thin, very sharp knife for cutting raw fish. Handle the fish as little as possible, by cutting each slice in a single motion, without sawing back and forth, as the friction will warm up the fish. Similarly, use the knife blade to lift or move slices on the cutting board or to place on the serving plate instead of your hands which will also warm up the fish.

Ideally, fish should be sliced as thinly as possible, and this is usually determined by the firmness of the fish. The firmer the fish, the thinner it can and should be sliced.

Ways of Cutting Fish

Paper-thin sashimi slices
Fish must be very fresh. Fillet can also be refrigerated for 10 minutes before slicing. Hold the fillet with one hand. Incline the knife at a 45° angle and slice very thinly but evenly, into strips that are about 3 mm ($^1/_8$ in) thick, working from the left to the right of the fillet.

Thin sushi slices
Cut the fillet crosswise into 3-mm to 6-mm ($^1/_8$-$^1/_4$-in) thick slices. Depending on the thickness of the fillet, these may be rectangular slices, bars or strips.

Cubes
Cut thick, soft-fleshed fish into 2-cm ($^3/_4$-in) cubes by cutting the fillet crosswise into 2-cm ($^3/_4$-in) strips, and then cutting these strips into 2-cm ($^3/_4$-in) pieces.

Strips
Cut very thin fillets diagonally or crosswise into strips that are 2 cm to 5 cm ($^3/_4$-2 in) wide and no longer than 5 cm (2 in) long. These strips (or threads) are then piled into a mound for serving.

How to Prepare Basic Sushi Rice

Although it is often referred to as glutinous or sticky rice, the rice most commonly eaten by the Japanese—*uruchi mai*—is non-glutinous. (The glutinous variety is known as *mochi gome*.) Short grain rice is readily available in supermarkets and usually includes the word "rose" in its name, e.g. "Japan Rose" or "California Rose", however it may simply be labeled "Japanese Rice". Uncooked Japanese rice, as with all other types of rice, should be stored in an airtight container at room temperature.

250 g (1 1/4 cups) uncooked short-grain Japanese rice
Cold water to wash rice
8-cm (3-in) square piece *konbu* (dried kelp)
300 ml (1 1/4 cups) water
1 tablespoon sake
1 tablespoon rice vinegar
1 tablespoon sugar
1 teaspoon salt

Makes 2 1/2 cups
Preparation time: **10 mins**
Cooking time: **15 mins**

1 Place the rice in a large bowl or saucepan and add enough cold water to cover. Stir the rice with your fingers for 1 minute until the water becomes quite cloudy. Drain in a colander and repeat the process 3 or 4 times until the water is almost clear. Drain in a colander and set aside for at least 1 hour.

2 Wipe the *konbu* with a damp cloth to remove any grit, but do not try to wipe off all the white powder. Using scissors, cut the *konbu* into 4 pieces.

3 Place the rice in a heavy saucepan or rice cooker. Add the water and sake, and place the *konbu* pieces on top. Cook over medium heat and remove the *konbu* just before it reaches boiling point (otherwise the rice becomes slimy). When the broth reaches a rolling boil, reduce heat to low, cover the saucepan, and simmer for about 15 minutes, or until all the liquid is absorbed. Try not to lift the lid too many times to check this.

4 Remove from the heat and leave the rice to sit covered for 15 minutes. Then, using a wooden spoon or rice paddle, gently fluff up the rice. Place a kitchen towel over the saucepan and cover with the lid. Leave for 10 minutes to absorb excess moisture. Dissolve the sugar and salt in the vinegar in a small, non-metal bowl. Spread the rice out to dry in a large, non-metal container, about 30 cm (12 in) across, and sprinkle the vinegar mixture over it.

5 Fold the vinegared rice gently with one hand while fanning the rice with the other. An electric fan can also be used. Continue fanning and folding the rice until it reaches room temperature, about 5 minutes. This quick cooling process is essential to achieve the desired texture, consistency and flavor of Sushi Rice.

6 Cover the container with a damp kitchen towel. The rice is now ready and can be kept at room temperature for up to 4 hours. Do not refrigerate the prepared Sushi Rice as this hardens and dries the grains.

Basic Dashi Stock (Bonito Flake Stock)

10-cm (4-in) square piece *konbu* (dried kelp), wiped clean
1 liter (4 cups) water
60 ml ($1/4$ cup) cold water
40 g (2 cups) bonito flakes

1 Cut the *konbu* into 4 uniform strips. Place in a saucepan with the water and cook over medium heat. Just before it boils, remove from the heat and discard the *konbu*.
2 Add the cold water and bonito flakes. Bring to a boil, then remove from the heat and set aside to cool.
3 When the bonito flakes have sunk to the bottom, strain the liquid and discard the flakes. Use as needed.

Basic Japanese Dips and Sauces

Soy Dipping Sauce

Soy sauce (preferably Japanese soy sauce)
Dash of sesame paste (page 5) or wasabi (optional)

1 Japanese-style soy is used as a basic dipping sauce for all types of Japanese food. It may also be mixed with a little sesame paste or wasabi.

Coriander Pesto

2 cloves garlic, peeled
30 g (1 oz) macadamia nuts or pine nuts
Juice from $1/2$ lemon
50 g (1 cup) coriander leaves (cilantro) and stems
Salt and black pepper, to taste
4 tablespoons oil

1 Combine the garlic, nuts, lemon juice, coriander leaves, salt and pepper, and process. Drizzle the oil through the funnel to form a smooth, light paste. Do not over process.
2 Pour into a clean airtight jar, smooth down the top, and cover surface with a thin layer of oil. Seal and refrigerate until required.

Homemade Japanese Mayonnaise

3 whole eggs
1 teaspoon Japanese mustard
Salt and black pepper to taste
3 tablespoons lime juice
1 clove garlic, crushed
500 ml (2 cups) light vegetable oil, not canola

1 Combine the eggs, mustard, salt, pepper, lime juice, and crushed garlic and process until light and frothy. Then gradually add the oil while processing, until the mayonnaise is thick.
2 Transfer to a storage jar, refrigerate, and use as required.

Ponzu Sauce

60 ml (1/4 cup) lemon juice
60 ml (1/4 cup) soy sauce
3 tablespoons Basic Dashi Stock (page 10) or 1/4 teaspoon instant *dashi* granules dissolved in 3 tablespoons boiling water
1 tablespoon *mirin*

1 Combine all the ingredients in a bowl and stir well.

Sesame Seed Sauce

100 g (3/4 cup) white sesame seeds, toasted
1 tablespoon miso
1 tablespoon sugar
2 tablespoons *mirin*
2 tablespoons rice vinegar
2 tablespoons sake
6 tablespoons soy sauce
1 teaspoon Japanese mustard
3 tablespoons Basic Dashi Stock (page 10) or 1/4 teaspoon instant *dashi* granules dissolved in 3 tablespoons boiling water

1 Combine all the ingredients in a bowl and blend until smooth.

Dips and Sauces 11

Healthy Miso Soup with Daikon

- 125 g (1 cup) daikon, peeled and sliced
- 1 liter (4 cups) Basic Dashi Stock (page 10) or 2 teaspoons instant *dashi* granules dissolved in 1 liter (4 cups) boiling water
- 3 tablespoons miso
- 8 green beans, cut into lengths
- 1 teaspoon soy sauce (optional)

1 Slice the daikon lengthwise into quarters, then into 3-mm ($1/_8$-in) slices as shown below.
2 Place the daikon and *dashi* stock in a saucepan over medium heat and cook until the daikon softens, about 2 minutes.
3 Place the miso in a small bowl and ladle some of the hot *dashi* stock over it. Stir with a wooden spoon until the miso is dissolved, and pour the dissolved miso into the soup.
4 Stir in the beans and soy sauce, then bring the soup to a boil and immediately remove from the heat. Ladle the soup into 4 bowls and serve.

Serves 4
Preparation time: **5 mins**
Cooking time: **5 mins**

1. Cut the daikon in quarters, lengthwise, then into 3-mm ($1/_8$-in) slices.

2. Cut the green beans into lengths.

3. Stir the miso and *dashi* stock with a wooden spoon until miso is well dissolved.

4. Stir in the beans and soy sauce, then bring to a boil and quickly remove from heat.

Flavorful Clear Soup with Prawns

- 8 medium prawns, peeled and deveined, tails intact
- 1 liter (4 cups) Basic Dashi Stock (page 10) or 2 teaspoons instant *dashi* granules dissolved in 1 liter (4 cups) boiling water
- 2 okra, cut in 1/2-cm (1/4-in) slices
- 1 teaspoon soy sauce
- 1 tablespoon finely grated lemon zest

1 Warm the *dashi* stock in a saucepan and adjust seasoning with salt, if required. Bring to a boil over medium heat and add the prawns. Reduce heat and simmer for 1 to 2 minutes, until the prawns turn pink. Add the okra and soy sauce and remove from the heat.
2 Place 2 prawns in each serving bowl and ladle the soup over them. Garnish each bowl with lemon zest and serve.

Serves 4
Preparation time: **15 mins**
Cooking time: **5 mins**

Miso Soup with Tofu and Mushrooms

- 1 liter (4 cups) Basic Dashi Stock (page 10) or 2 teaspoons instant *dashi* granules dissolved in 1 liter (4 cups) boiling water
- 4 fresh shiitake mushrooms, stems discarded, caps cut into 1 cm ($1/2$ in) sections,
- 200 g (7 oz) soft tofu, cubed
- 4 tablespoons miso
- Soy sauce to taste

1 Bring the *dashi* stock almost to a boil in a saucepan and add the sliced mushrooms. Reduce heat and simmer the mushrooms for 1 minute, then add the tofu. Reduce heat to very low.

2 Place the miso in a small bowl and ladle some of the hot *dashi* stock over it. Stir with a wooden spoon until the miso is well dissolved. Pour the dissolved miso into the saucepan.

3 Stir in the soy sauce and return the soup to almost a boil. Remove from the heat immediately, ladle the soup into 4 soup bowls, and serve.

Serves 4
Preparation time: **20 mins**
Cooking time: **10 mins**

Traditional Seafood Sashimi Platter

½ small daikon, peeled and grated into thin threads to yield 75 g (½ cup)
Ice water
4 *shiso* leaves or other leafy greens
50 g (2 oz) green seaweed or salted greens, to garnish (optional)
150 g (5 oz) fresh tuna fillet, skinned
150 g (5 oz) fresh sea bream fillet or mackerel, skinned
1 fresh abalone or giant clam, shucked and cleaned
150 g (5 oz) fresh squid, skinned and cleaned
4 fresh scallops, about 85 g (3 oz)
150 g (5 oz) boiled octopus
1 tablespoon wasabi paste
4 tablespoons soy sauce or Ponzu Sauce (page 11)

1 Peel the daikon and leave it in the ice water until needed. Drain well before serving. Rinse the *shiso* leaves and seaweed in cold water. Pat dry with paper toweling.
2 To prepare the fish, trim the thin sides of the tuna and sea bream fillet to make a more rectangular shape if necessary. Cut into thin slices. Cut the abalone crosswise into ½-cm (¼-in) slices. Open the squid flat. Make cuts along the body about 5 cm (2 in) apart to make rectangles. Cut these rectangles across to make thin strips.
3 Slice the scallops to make 5 thin discs. Slice the boiled octopus into ½-cm (¼-in) slices.
4 Arrange all the seafood, garnish and wasabi paste on a serving platter. Pour the dipping sauce into small individual dipping bowls and serve immediately.

Boiled octopus is available precooked in Japanese supermarkets. If fresh octopus is used, simmer for about 1 to 1½ hours in a pot of lightly-salted water until tender

Serves 4
Preparation time: **30 mins**
Assembling time: **5 mins**

Pickled Ginger

- 125 g ($^1/_2$ cup) fresh young ginger, peeled and thinly sliced diagonally
- 250 ml (1 cup) boiling water
- 125 ml ($^1/_2$ cup) rice vinegar
- 2 tablespoons sugar
- $^1/_2$ teaspoon salt

1 Place the ginger slices in a small bowl and cover with the boiling water. Leave to stand for 30 seconds and drain well.
2 Combine the vinegar, sugar and salt in a small non-metallic bowl and stir until the sugar completely dissolves. Add the drained ginger and coat well with the mixture.
3 Cover the bowl with a plastic sheet and leave it to stand for at least 1 hour, then refrigerate until well-chilled and the ginger slices turn pink. To serve, remove the ginger from the pickling liquid.

Simple Tuna Sashimi

- 1 teaspoon wasabi paste
- Juice from 2 large limes
- 450 g (1 lb) fresh tuna fillet, thinly sliced
- 75 g ($^1/_2$ cup) grated daikon
- 4 tablespoons Pickled Ginger (see above)
- 4 sprigs fresh coriander leaves (cilantro)

1 To prepare the dressing, mix the wasabi paste with the lime juice and set aside.
2 To arrange the sashimi, distribute the slices of tuna onto 4 individual serving plates. Garnish with a small mound of the radish, topped with the Pickled Ginger. Sprinkle the tuna with the fresh coriander leaves and drizzle with the prepared dressing. Serve immediately.

Serves 4
Preparation time: **1 hour**
Assembling time: **5 mins**

Tuna with Daikon

250 g (8 oz) lean fresh tuna
1 tablespoon sesame paste (page 5)
125 g (4 oz/1 cup) daikon, sliced into matchsticks
Soy Dipping Sauce or Ponzu Sauce (pages 10–11)

Serves 2
Preparation time: **15 mins**

1 Slice the tuna 3 mm ($1/8$ in) thick. Cut each slice into strips 2 cm ($3/4$ in) wide.
2 Spread the sesame paste on 1 side of each tuna strip.
3 To assemble, line up 1 tablespoon of the daikon evenly so that the sticks are parallel. Hold the daikon with the fingertips of one hand and wrap the tuna around the base of the daikon. The side of the tuna strip with sesame paste should face inside, touching the daikon. The tops of the daikon sticks should stand out slightly above the tuna wrap.
4 Stand the sashimi on a serving platter and serve with either Soy Dipping Sauce or Ponzu Sauce.

Squid with Nori

250 g (8 oz) squid, skinned, cleaned, and tentacles removed
2 sheets *nori*, toasted (page 42)
Soy Dipping Sauce or Ponzu Sauce (pages 10–11)

Serves 2
Preparation time: **15 mins**

1 Flatten the squid and insert the sharp point of a knife through the top of the sack, pulling the knife towards you to open the squid. Remove any fat and skin.
2 Cut the squid halves into six 6 x $7^1/_2$-cm ($2^1/_2$ x 3-in) rectangles. Cut each rectangle into uniform strips, about 2 cm ($3/4$ in) wide.
3 Using scissors, cut the *nori* into strips to exactly fit the squid strips.
4 Layer 3 strips of the squid alternating with 2 strips of the *nori*, beginning and ending with the squid. Cut the stack crosswise into 3 or 4 equal slices and serve with either Soy Dipping Sauce or Ponzu Sauce.

Nigiri Sushi with Prawns, Tuna and Eel

6 medium prawns, peeled and deveined, tails intact
Small bowl ice water
60 ml (1/4 cup) rice vinegar
2 teaspoons sugar
250 g (8 oz) fresh tuna fillet, skinned
250 g (8 oz) smoked conger eel (*anago*, page 5)
Small bowl *tezu* (page 5)
300 g (2 cups) cooked Sushi Rice (pages 8–9)
2 tablespoons wasabi paste
Pickled Ginger (page 18)
Soy Dipping Sauce (page 10)

Serves 4
Preparation time: **30 mins**
Assembling time: **40 mins**

1 Bring a saucepan of salted water to a boil. Insert a wooden skewer lengthwise into each prawn from end to end to prevent the prawns from curling during blanching. Blanch the prawns for 30 seconds. Remove immediately and refresh in ice water.
2 Combine the vinegar and sugar in a small bowl. Add the prawns and let stand for 5 minutes, then drain.
3 Slide a knife lengthwise along the underside of the prawn without cutting through. Open the prawn flat, top side up; repeat with the remaining prawns. Pat dry with paper toweling.
4 Cut the tuna fillet crosswise into 2 x 5-cm (1 x 2-in) pieces. Cut the eel into thin slices.
5 To shape the rice, first moisten hands with the *tezu* to avoid sticking, then take 1 tablespoon of the Sushi Rice in your right hand and shape to form an oval "finger". Pick up the tuna with your left hand and use your right index finger to dab a little wasabi on it. Place the rice "finger" on top of the tuna. Using your index finger, press the rice onto the tuna. Turn the rice and tuna over so that the tuna is on top. Using your index finger and middle finger, mold the tuna around the rice so that the rice does not show around the edges of the tuna. Repeat with the remaining tuna, prawns and eel.
6 Arrange the Nigiri Sushi on a serving platter. Serve with Pickled Ginger and Soy Dipping Sauce.

Nigiri Sushi with Egg

Rolled Omelet
- 4 large eggs
- 5 tablespoons Basic Dashi Stock (page 10) or 1/4 teaspoon instant *dashi* granules dissolved in 5 tablespoons boiling water
- 2 tablespoons *mirin*
- 1 teaspoon sugar
- Scant 1 teaspoon soy sauce
- 1/4 teaspoon salt
- Oil for frying

Sushi
- 300 g (2 cups) cooked Sushi Rice (pages 8–9)
- 1 sheet *nori*, toasted (page 42) and cut into 1-cm (1/2-in) strips
- Small bowl *tezu* (page 5)

Serves 4
Preparation time: **20 mins**
Cooking time: **15 mins**

1 To make the omelet, gently combine the eggs in a bowl with the *dashi* stock, *mirin*, sugar, soy sauce and salt. Stir until the sugar is dissolved.

2 Heat a regular skillet or omelet pan over medium heat and brush it lightly with the oil. Pour about one-third of the egg mixture into the skillet, tilting the skillet to cover the base. When the egg is set on the bottom but still moist on top, about 30 seconds, use a spatula or chopsticks to roll the egg up quickly but carefully. Leave the rolled omelet on one side of the skillet.

3 Brush the skillet with more of the oil and pour half of the remaining egg mixture into the skillet, again tilting the pan to cover the base. After 30 seconds, roll out the first omelet over the new one. Repeat with the remaining egg mixture.

4 Lift the final omelet onto a bamboo mat or kitchen towel and roll it up, gently squeezing out any excess moisture. Let it stand for 1 to 2 minutes. Serve immediately, garnished with sliced daikon mixed with a little soy, or use as a topping for sushi.

5 To use as a sushi topping, place the prepared rolled omelet on a board and flatten it slightly to make it more rectangular. Cut it crosswise into 1-cm (1/2-in) slices.

6 Moisten hands with the *tezu*. Form rice "fingers" as in page 22. Repeat method of making sushi, using the omelet as the topping until all the Sushi Rice is used up.

7 Dampen 1 end of a *nori* strip and wrap it around the sushi like a belt. Repeat with the remaining ingredients.

1. Using a spatula or chopsticks, roll up the omelet to one side of the pan.

2. Pour new egg mixture into the pan then roll back the omelet in this new egg mixture.

Hand-formed Nigiri Sushi

Inari Tofu Pouch Sushi

- 6 deep-fried tofu slices (*abura-age*, page 3)
- 250 ml (1 cup) Basic Dashi Stock (page 10) or 1/2 teaspoon instant *dashi* granules dissolved in 250 ml (1 cup) boiling water
- 2 tablespoons sake
- 2 tablespoons soy sauce
- 1 1/2 tablespoons sugar
- 1 tablespoon *mirin*
- Small bowl *tezu* (page 5)
- 300 g (2 cups) cooked Sushi Rice (pages 8–9)
- Black or white sesame seeds, toasted
- 4 tablespoons Pickled Ginger (page 18)
- Soy Dipping Sauce (page 10)

1 Rinse the deep-fried tofu slices under boiling water for a few seconds to remove excess oil. Drain and pat dry with paper toweling.

2 Heat the *dashi* stock, sake, soy sauce, sugar and *mirin* in a saucepan and bring to a boil. Reduce heat, add the tofu slices and simmer for 10 minutes. Remove from the heat and drain.

3 Cut the tofu slices in half, either diagonally or crosswise, depending on the desired shape.

4 Moisten hands with the *tezu* to prevent rice from sticking. Open the tofu pouch and carefully insert 2 tablespoons of the Sushi Rice. Fold the edges of the pouch over the rice to seal it and place it seam side down on a serving plate.

5 Sprinkle with the sesame seeds and serve with the Pickled Ginger and Soy Dipping Sauce.

Makes 12 pouches
Preparation time: **10 mins**
Cooking time: **5 mins**
Assembling time: **10 mins**

1. Remove the tofu slices from the simmering liquid with a slotted spoon.

2. Slice the simmered tofu crosswise or diagonally.

3. Open the tofu pouch carefully and fill it with a little Sushi Rice.

4. Fold the edges of the pouch to seal it, then place it seam side down on a plate.

Crab Salad Tofu Pouch

- 6 deep-fried tofu slices (*abura-age*, page 3)
- 250 ml (1 cup) Basic Dashi Stock (page 10) or 1/2 teaspoon instant *dashi* granules dissolved in 250 ml (1 cup) boiling water
- 2 tablespoons sake
- 2 tablespoons soy sauce
- 1 1/2 tablespoons sugar
- 1 tablespoon *mirin*
- 250 g (8 oz) cooked crab meat, picked clean
- 125 ml (1/2 cup) Homemade Japanese Mayonnaise (page 11)
- 1/2 avocado, diced and sprinkled with lemon juice
- 2 to 3 water chestnuts, diced
- 2 tablespoons salmon roe or flying fish roe
- Soy Dipping Sauce (page 10)

1 Rinse the tofu slices in boiling water for a few seconds to remove excess oil. Drain and pat dry with paper toweling.
2 Heat the *dashi* stock, sake, soy sauce, sugar and *mirin* in a saucepan and bring to a boil. Reduce heat, add the tofu and simmer for 10 minutes. Remove from the heat, drain and allow the tofu to cool completely.
3 Cut the tofu slices in half, either diagonally or crosswise, depending on the desired shape.
4 Squeeze out any excess liquid from the crab meat and combine with the mayonnaise. Pat dry the avocado and water chestnuts before combining with the crab mixture and the salmon roe. Gently fold the salad, taking care not to break up the delicate ingredients.
5 Insert 2 teaspoons of the crab salad into the tofu pouch. Flatten the base of the pouches and sit them upright on a serving platter.

Makes 12 pouches
Preparation time: **10 mins**
Cooking time: **5 mins**
Assembling time: **10 mins**

Cucumber, Crab and Salmon Sushi Rolls

1 small cucumber, peeled
3 sheets *nori*, toasted (page 42) and halved
Small bowl *tezu* (page 5)
450 g (3 cups) cooked Sushi Rice (pages 8–9)
2 tablespoons wasabi paste
2 tablespoons white sesame seeds, toasted
250 g (8 oz) salmon fillet, skinned and cut into thin strips
250 g (8 oz) cooked crab meat or crab sticks
90 ml (1/3 cup) soy sauce
3/4 cup Pickled Ginger (page 18)

Serves 4
Preparation time: **20 mins**
Assembling time: **30 mins**

1 To make the cucumber rolls, halve, then quarter the cucumber lengthwise into thin, long strips.

2 Place the bamboo mat on a work surface, facing you with the strips horizontal. Place a half sheet of the *nori* on the mat, shiny side down, with the edge of the *nori* 2 cm (3/4 in) away from the edge of the mat closer to you.

3 To make the rolls, moisten your hands with the *tezu* to prevent the rice from sticking. Spread about 75 g (1/2 cup) of the Sushi Rice onto the *nori* with your fingers, leaving a 2 cm (3/4 in) space at the top of the *nori* sheet.

4 Dab some of the wasabi paste down the middle of the rice and place 2 to 3 pieces of the cucumber on the wasabi. Sprinkle 1 teaspoon of the sesame seeds on the rice.

5 To roll, hold the edge of the mat nearest to you with one hand, press fingers of the other hand over the cucumber to hold it in place and roll the mat over the rice, away from you. Lift up the top of the mat and turn the roll over a little so that the empty *nori* strip seals the sushi roll.

6 Unroll the bamboo mat and remove the sushi roll. Using a moist, very sharp knife, cut the roll into 6 to 8 uniform pieces. Repeat using the salmon and crab meat. Serve with the soy sauce and Pickled Ginger.

1. Place the nori *on the bamboo mat 1 1/2 cm (3/4 in) away from the edge closer to you.*

2. Spread the rice evenly over the nori*, leaving a 2 cm (3/4 in) gap at the top.*

3. Roll the bamboo mat over the rice, away from you.

4. Using a moist, very sharp knife, cut the roll into 6 to 8 pieces.

Smoked Eel and Avocado Sushi Rolls

1 whole ripe avocado, peeled and pitted
Juice from 1 lemon
3 sheets *nori*, toasted (page 42)
Small bowl *tezu* (page 5)
450 g (3 cups) cooked Sushi Rice (pages 8–9)
1/2 cup *furikake* (topping for rice, see page 3)
250 g (1/2 lb) smoked conger eel (page 5), skinned and deboned or smoked trout or kippers

1 Slice the avocado lengthwise into 1-cm (1/2-in) strips, place on a flat dish and drizzle with the lemon juice to prevent discoloring.
2 Place a bamboo mat in front of you, strips horizontal. Place 1 sheet of the *nori* on the mat, shiny side down with the edge of the *nori* 2 cm (3/4 in) away from the edge of the mat closer to you.
3 To make the rolls, moisten hands with the *tezu* to prevent the rice from sticking. Spread 1 cup of the Sushi Rice evenly onto the *nori* with your fingers, leaving a 2 cm (3/4 in) space at the top of the *nori*. Sprinkle the rice with some of the *furikake*.
4 Lay strips of the smoked eel and avocado down the middle of the rice.
5 Roll the mat as in the sushi rolls (page 30). Shape the roll into a square and cut into 8 uniform slices. Repeat with the remaining *nori*, eel and avocado slices.

Makes 24 slices
Preparation time: **10 mins**

California Rolls

12 medium prawns, peeled and deveined or 1 cup cooked crab meat
1 large avocado
Juice from half a lemon
4 sheets *nori*, toasted (page 42)
600 g (4 cups) cooked Sushi Rice (pages 8–9)
8 lettuce leaves, coarsely cut
3 tablespoons Homemade Japanese Mayonnaise (page 11) mixed with 1 teaspoon wasabi paste
3 tablespoons Pickled Ginger (page 18)
3 tablespoons salmon roe
1 tablespoon toasted sesame seeds

1 Poach the prawns and set aside to cool.
2 Cut the avocado in half lengthwise. Remove the flesh and cut into strips about 1 cm ($1/2$ in) thick, keeping the pieces as long as possible. Drizzle with the lemon juice to prevent discoloration.
3 To make the rolls, follow the directions for rolling sushi on page 30. Place 2 lettuce leaves down the middle of the rice on each roll. Top with 3 prawns, placing them end to end along the center of the lettuce. Place the avocado strips end to end to form a line next to the prawns.
4 Spoon $1/4$ of the mayonnaise on the prawns and add some of the Pickled Ginger, salmon roe and sesame seeds to the roll. Roll up like the sushi rolls on page 30 and cut each roll into 8 slices.

Makes 32 slices
Preparation time: **15 mins**
Assembling time: **30 mins**

Ocean Trout California Rolls

- 200 g (8 oz) ocean trout fillets
- 1/2 cup pickled Chinese olives vegetable (page 4)
- 600 g (4 cups) cooked Sushi Rice (pages 8–9)
- 4 sheets *nori*, toasted (page 42)
- 2 tablespoons sliced capers
- Dill cucumbers, peeled and cut into thin strips
- 3 tablespoons Homemade Japanese Mayonnaise (page 11)
- 1 tablespoon Dijon mustard

1 Cut the ocean trout fillet into strips about 2 cm (3/4 in) thick.
2 Mix the olives into the Sushi Rice.
3 Follow the directions for making California Rolls (page 35), using the dill cucumbers, mayonnaise and Dijon mustard as a filling.

Makes 32 slices
Preparation time: **20 mins**
Assembling time: **30 mins**

Thai Prawn California Rolls

- 12 medium prawns, peeled and deveined
- 2 tablespoons lemon juice
- 2 tablespoons fish sauce
- 1 tablespoon palm sugar (page 4)
- 1 spring onion, thinly sliced
- 1 small chili, thinly sliced
- 600 g (4 cups) cooked Sushi Rice (pages 8–9)
- 4 sheets *nori*, toasted (page 42)
- 8 lettuce leaves, roughly sliced
- Japanese cucumber, unpeeled and cut into strips
- 1/2 cup fresh coriander leaves (cilantro)

1 Marinate the prawns in the lemon juice, fish sauce, palm sugar, spring onion and chili for 15 minutes.
2 Follow the directions for making California Rolls (page 35). Drain off excess liquid from the lettuce and place it over the middle of the prepared rice.
3 Place 3 prawns end to end along the center of the rice, then add a strip of the Japanese cucumber and sprinkle with the fresh coriander leaves. Repeat until all the ingredients are used up.

Makes 32 slices
Preparation time: **20 mins**
Assembling time: **30 mins**

Lobster and Mango California Rolls

4 sheets *nori*, toasted (page 42)
600 g (4 cups) cooked Sushi Rice (pages 8–9)
1 cup cooked lobster meat
$1/2$ firm mango, sliced
3 tablespoons Homemade Japanese Mayonnaise (page 11)
1 tablespoon Thai chili sauce
25 g (1 cup) mint leaves

1 Follow the directions for making California Rolls on page 35 using lobster meat, mango, mayonnaise, chili sauce and mint as the filling.

Makes 32 slices
Preparation time: **20 mins**
Assembling time: **30 mins**

Battleship Gunkan Sushi

6 fresh scallops, cut into small cubes
2 tablespoons sake
1 spring onion, diced
Oil for grilling scallops
Small bowl *tezu* (page 5)
300 g (2 cups) cooked Sushi Rice (pages 8–9)
4 sheets *nori*, toasted (page 42) and cut into $2^1/_2$-cm (1-in) strips
125 g (4 oz) salmon or *tobiko* roe
125 g (4 oz) seasoned jellyfish (page 5), or fresh minced tuna
60 g (2 oz) seasoned *wakame* seaweed (page 5), or smoked oysters
80 g (3 oz) fresh or canned clams

1 Marinate the scallops in the sake and spring onion for 15 minutes. Remove scallops and drain.
2 Meanwhile, heat a grill and brush with the oil. Cook the scallops for 2 minutes on both sides. Remove from the heat and, when cool, cut the grilled scallops into 1-cm ($^1/_2$-in) cubes.
3 Moisten hands with the *tezu*. Take 1 tablespoon of the Sushi Rice and form into an oval shape. Place the rice oval on a flat surface and wrap a strip of the *nori* around its sides, leaving the top and bottom uncovered. The *nori* should be about 1 cm ($^1/_2$ in) taller than the rice it is wrapped around, and resemble a battleship.
4 Continue shaping the remaining rice, wrapping each rice oval with a strip of *nori*.
5 Spoon the cooked scallop onto 6 of the sushi. Repeat with the salmon roe, seasoned jellyfish, seaweed and clams to make 30 battleships in all.

Serves 4
Preparation time: **30 mins**
Assembling time: **30 mins**

Chicken Teriyaki Battleship Sushi

- 2 tablespoons soy sauce
- 2 tablespoons sake
- 1 teaspoon sugar
- 200 g (7 oz) chicken breast, skin removed and sliced into 2-cm ($3/4$-in) strips
- Small bowl *tezu* (page 5)
- 300 g (2 cups) cooked Sushi Rice (pages 8–9)
- 4 sheets *nori*, toasted (page 42) and cut into 2-cm (1-in) strips

1 Combine the soy sauce, sake and sugar in a small bowl and add the chicken strips. Marinate for 15 to 30 minutes. Drain the chicken.

2 Grill or broil the chicken over high heat for 1 minute on each side. Remove from the heat and leave to cool to room temperature.

3 Follow steps 3 through 5 for preparing Battleship Gunkan Sushi on page 39.

4 When the chicken is cold, slice it very thin and arrange on top of the sushi to form battleships.

Serves 4
Preparation time: **30 mins**
Cooking time: **2 mins**
Assembling time: **15 mins**

Red Salmon Battleship Sushi

- 1 can (185 g/6 oz) salmon
- 3 tablespoons Homemade Japanese Mayonnaise (page 11)
- 1/4 teaspoon salt
- 1/4 teaspoon freshly ground black pepper
- 1 Japanese cucumber
- Small bowl *tezu* (page 5)
- 300 g (2 cups) cooked Sushi Rice (pages 8–9)
- 4 sheets *nori*, toasted (page 42) and cut into 2-cm (1-in) strips

1 Drain the salmon and remove any skin and bones.
2 In a small bowl, mix the mayonnaise with the salmon, salt and black pepper. Do not overmix.
3 Slice the cucumber into very fine transparent circles. Place it on paper toweling and pat dry to remove excess moisture.
4 Follow steps 3 through 5 for preparing Battleship Gunkan Sushi on page 39.
5 Spoon the salmon filling on the battleships. Top with the sliced cucumber to completely cover the fish.

Serves 4
Preparation time: **20 mins**
Assembling time: **15 mins**

Hand-rolled Cone Temaki Sushi

3 sheets *nori*, toasted (see photo below)
Small bowl *tezu* (page 5)
300 g (2 cups) cooked Sushi Rice (pages 8–9)
1 tablespoon wasabi paste
10 *shiso* leaves
1 Japanese cucumber, cut into 8-cm (3-in) lengths
150 g (5 oz) fresh salmon fillet, cut into 12 strips
1 Rolled Omelet (page 24) cut into 12 strips
60 g (2 oz) salmon roe
Pickled Ginger (page 18)
Soy Dipping Sauce (page 10)

1 After toasting the *nori* as shown below, cut it into 4 squares. Place 1 *nori* square diagonally in your left hand, shiny side facing down.

2 To make the rolls, moisten right hand with the *tezu* to prevent the rice from sticking. Place 2 tablespoons of the Sushi Rice on the *nori* square. Spread a dab of the wasabi paste on the rice, then a *shiso* leaf and top with the cucumber, salmon, omelet and salmon roe. Fold the edges of the *nori* towards the center to form a cone-shaped roll. Use a little water to seal the *nori*. Repeat with the remaining *nori* and all the other ingredients.

3 Serve with Pickled Ginger and Soy Dipping Sauce.

Serves 4
Preparation time: **15 mins**
Assembling time: **15 mins**

1. Toast the nori by holding it over a gas flame for about 30 seconds. It will change from black to a dark but bright green color.

2. Place the nori *square diagonally in your left hand, shiny side facing down.*

3. Place the various toppings over the rice on top of the nori.

4. Fold the edges of the nori *in to form a cone-shaped roll.*

Temaki Sushi with Garlic Ginger Chicken

2 tablespoons oil
2 large cloves garlic, crushed
3 cm (1 1/2 in) fresh ginger, thinly sliced
2 small red chilies, deseeded and finely diced
1/2 cup finely diced water chestnuts
200 g (7 oz) chicken breast, skin removed and cut into thin, long strips
1 teaspoon sake
1 teaspoon salt
1/4 teaspoon freshly ground black pepper
1/4 teaspoon fish sauce
1/2 teaspoon sesame oil
2 spring onions, sliced at an angle
3 sheets *nori*, toasted (page 42)
Small bowl *tezu* (page 5)
300 g (2 cups) cooked Sushi Rice (pages 8–9)
Pickled Ginger (page 18)
Soy Dipping Sauce (page 10)

1 Heat the oil in a wok over medium heat and stir-fry the garlic, ginger and chilies for 5 seconds. Add the water chestnuts and chicken.

2 Toss the ingredients in the wok until the chicken is just cooked. Remove from the heat and drain. Place the cooked food into a bowl, season with sake, salt, pepper, fish sauce and sesame oil, and set aside to cool. When completely cold, stir in the spring onions and mix well.

3 Cut the *nori* sheets into 4 squares. Place 1 *nori* square diagonally in your left hand, shiny side facing down.

4 To make the rolls, moisten right hand with the *tezu* to prevent the rice from sticking. Place 2 tablespoons of the Sushi Rice on the *nori* square. Spoon 2 tablespoons of the chicken mixture on top of the rice and fold the edges of the *nori* in to form a cone-shaped roll. Use a little water to seal the *nori*. Repeat with the remaining ingredients.

5 Serve with Pickled Ginger and Soy Dipping Sauce.

Serves 4
Preparation time: **10 mins**
Cooking time: **20 mins**

Temaki Sushi with Asparagus and Smoked Trout

3 sheets *nori*, toasted (page 42)
1 smoked trout, skinned and deboned
1 tablespoon wasabi paste
125 ml ($1/2$ cup) Homemade Japanese Mayonnaise (page 11)
$1/4$ teaspoon salt
$1/4$ teaspoon freshly ground black pepper
6 stalks fresh asparagus, trimmed and cooked
Small bowl *tezu* (page 5)
300 g (2 cups) cooked Sushi Rice (pages 8–9)
Soy Dipping Sauce (page 10)

1 Cut the toasted *nori* into 4 squares.
2 Combine the smoked trout, wasabi, mayonnaise, salt and black pepper in a mixing bowl.
3 Trim the asparagus spears into 8-cm (3-in) lengths and cut in half crosswise to make 12 pieces.
4 Place a *nori* square diagonally in your left hand, shiny side facing down. To make the rolls, moisten right hand with the *tezu* to prevent the rice from sticking. Place 2 tablespoons of the Sushi Rice on the *nori* square. Put 1 piece of the asparagus down the center of the rice and add 2 tablespoons of the trout mixture. Fold the edges of the *nori* in to form a cone-shaped roll. Seal with a little water. Repeat with the remaining ingredients.
5 Serve with Soy Dipping Sauce.

Serves 4
Preparation time: **10 mins**
Assembling time: **20 mins**

Mixed Vegetables on Sushi Rice

Kanpyo
- 30 g (1 oz) *kanpyo* (dried gourd strips)
- 250 ml (1 cup) Basic Dashi Stock (page 10) or 1/2 teaspoon instant *dashi* granules dissolved in 250 ml (1 cup) boiling water
- 2 tablespoons soy sauce
- 1 tablespoon *mirin*

Sushi
- 6 dried or fresh shiitake mushrooms
- 2 slices deep-fried tofu (*abura-age*, see page 3)
- 1 section (125 g/4 oz) fresh lotus root, peeled
- 1 teaspoon vinegar
- 1 medium carrot
- 125 ml (1/2 cup) Basic Dashi Stock (page 10) or 1/4 teaspoon instant *dashi* granules dissolved in 125 ml (1/2 cup) boiling water
- 1 1/2 tablespoons sugar
- 1/2 teaspoon salt
- 1 1/2 tablespoons soy sauce
- 1 tablespoon *mirin*
- 750 g (5 cups) cooked Sushi Rice (pages 8–9)

Garnish
- 1 Sesame Omelet (page 52), cut in strips
- 60 g (2 oz) snow peas, thinly sliced
- 1/2 sheet *nori*, toasted (page 42) and shredded
- Pickled Ginger (page 18)

1 If using dried mushrooms, soften them in hot water, about 20 minutes.

2 Rinse the dried gourd in cold water. Mix the gourd with a little salt and rub it between your hands to soften, and rinse in cold water again. Place the gourd in a saucepan and cover with cold water. Bring to a boil over medium-high heat and cook for 10 minutes. Drain.

3 Place the *dashi* stock, soy sauce, sugar, *mirin* and the gourd into a saucepan and bring to a boil over medium to high heat. Reduce heat to low and cook until the gourd is tender and slightly translucent, about 20 minutes. Most of the liquid will be absorbed. Drain and set aside. When cool enough to handle, cut the gourd into 2-cm (3/4-in) pieces.

4 Drain the mushrooms and squeeze out excess moisture, reserving 125 ml (1/2 cup) of the liquid. Discard the stems and slice the mushroom caps thinly.

5 Rinse the tofu slices in boiling water in a colander to remove excess oil. Drain, then pat dry with paper toweling. Cut each piece lengthwise in half, then slice each half into thin strips.

6 Cut the lotus root into thin slices. If the root is large, cut the slices into 2-cm (3/4-in) strips. Soak strips in 1 cup of water mixed with the vinegar for 5 minutes. Drain and set aside.

7 Cut the carrot lengthwise into quarters. Cut each quarter into 2-cm (3/4-in) pieces. Turn the flat side of the carrot onto a board and cut into very thin slices.

8 Heat the reserved mushroom liquid with the *dashi* stock, sugar, salt, soy sauce and *mirin*. Add mushrooms, tofu, lotus root and carrot, and cook until tender, about 10 minutes. Remove from the heat and drain.

9 To assemble and serve, carefully stir the gourd and vegetables with the Sushi Rice. Do not overmix. Place the rice mixture into individual serving bowls and arrange small amounts of each garnish on top.

Serves 4
Preparation time: **45 mins**
Cooking time: **10 mins**

Sesame Spinach Sushi

4 large eggs
1/2 teaspoon salt
1/2 teaspoon freshly ground black pepper
2 tablespoons oil
2 hard-boiled eggs, shelled and diced
150 g (1 cup) cooked Sushi Rice (pages 8–9)
1/4 teaspoon salt
1/4 teaspoon freshly ground black pepper
1/2 sheet *nori*, toasted (see page 42), cut into 6 strips

Sesame Spinach
2 tablespoons white sesame seeds, toasted
300 g (10 oz/4 cups) fresh spinach leaves
1/2 teaspoon sugar
Large pinch of salt
2 tablespoons *Dashi* Stock (page 10) or 1/4 teaspoon instant *dashi* granules dissolved in 2 tablespoons boiling water
1 tablespoon soy sauce

1 Wash the spinach leaves and set aside to drain.
2 To prepare the Sesame Spinach, grind the sesame seeds until smooth with a mortar and pestle. Heat the sugar, salt, *dashi* stock, soy sauce and the ground seeds in a large saucepan over high heat. Toss in the spinach, one handful at a time until all the spinach is just cooked. Remove from the heat and drain. Set aside to use as a filling for the sushi, or serve immediately as a side dish garnished with toasted sesame seeds.
3 To make the egg wrappers for the sushi, mix the eggs, salt and pepper together in a bowl. Cook one-sixth of the egg mixture in an omelet pan using 1 teaspoon of oil. Do the same with the rest of the egg mixture to make 6 small omelets. Stack the omelets on top of each other and cover with a cloth to prevent them from drying out.
4 Combine the diced hard-boiled eggs and spinach with the Sushi Rice. Season with salt and black pepper.
5 Place the omelets flat on a work surface and spoon 2 tablespoons of the egg and spinach mixture onto each. Gather up the edges of the omelet and tie with a thin strip of *nori* to form a parcel. Repeat to form 6 parcels.

Makes 6 parcels
Preparation time: **20 mins**
Cooking time: **20 mins**

1. Grind sesame seeds in a mortar and pestle until smooth.

2. Add the spinach to the saucepan a handful at a time, stirring constantly.

Egg-wrapped Sushi 51

Sesame Omelet

2 large eggs
$1/4$ teaspoon salt
$1/4$ teaspoon freshly ground black pepper
1 tablespoon oil
2 tablespoons white or black sesame seeds

Makes 1 large omelet
Preparation time: **5 mins**
Cooking time: **5 mins**

1 Gently combine the eggs in a bowl with the salt and pepper. Do not overmix as this will make the omelet tough.
2 Using a pastry brush, lightly brush the inside of a large omelet pan with the oil. Heat the omelet pan over medium heat and pour in the egg mixture.
3 Tilt the pan to cover the bottom with the egg, and using a spatula, swirl the egg around to allow it to cook.
4 When the omelet is almost set, sprinkle with the sesame seeds. Flip the omelet over and allow the seeds to toast for 1 minute.
5 Slide the omelet from the pan onto a plate or cutting board.

Sesame Omelet with Prawns

10 medium prawns, peeled and deveined
250 ml (1 cup) water
3 tablespoons Homemade Japanese Mayonnaise (page 11)
$1/2$ teaspoon freshly ground black pepper
1 Sesame Omelet (see above)
$1/2$ teaspoon fish sauce
4 sprigs watercress

Makes 10–12 slices
Preparation time: **5 mins**
Cooking time: **10 mins**
Assembling time: **10 mins**

1 Boil the prawns in the water for 3 to 4 minutes, until they turn pink. Remove and let cool. Slice the prawns into small chunks and mix with the mayonnaise and black pepper.
2 Lay the Sesame Omelet on a flat work surface and spread the prawn mixture across the center of the omelet. Sprinkle the fish sauce over the prawn mixture, and place the watercress sprigs in a line across the middle.
3 Carefully roll up the omelet. Wrap it in plastic wrap and refrigerate for about 10 minutes to help it retain its shape before slicing into 10 or 12 pieces.

Egg-wrapped Sushi with Mushrooms

- 4 dried or fresh shiitake mushrooms
- 2 batches Sesame Omelet (page 52), omitting sesame seeds
- 1 clove garlic, crushed
- 2 tablespoons soy sauce
- 150 g (1 cup) cooked Sushi Rice (pages 8–9)
- 1 spring onion, sliced
- 1/4 teaspoon salt
- 1/4 teaspoon freshly ground black pepper

Makes 6 parcels
Preparation time: **20 mins**
Cooking time: **20 mins**
Assembling time: **15 mins**

1 If using dried mushrooms, soak them in hot water to soften, about 20 minutes. Drain the mushrooms and squeeze out any excess moisture.

2 Make 6 small omelets in a small skillet. Stack the omelets on top of each other and cover with a cloth to prevent them from drying out.

3 Discard the mushroom stems and dice the caps. Combine the garlic and soy sauce in a bowl and marinate the mushroom for at least 15 minutes.

4 Drain the mushrooms and combine with the Sushi Rice and spring onion in a mixing bowl. Season with the salt and black pepper.

5 Place the omelets on a flat work surface and spoon 2 tablespoons of the mushroom-rice mixture onto each one. Fold in the sides to form a flat, square parcel and place seam side down on a serving platter.

1. Make the omelets in a small skillet.

2. Discard the stems and dice the mushroom caps.

3. Combine the rice, diced mushrooms, salt and black pepper in a small bowl.

4. Fold in the sides of the omelet to form a flat, square parcel; place it seam side down.

Shiitake Mushroom Rolls

6 fresh shiitake mushrooms, stems discarded
1 teaspoon soy sauce
1 teaspoon sesame oil
1 teaspoon lemon juice
1 teaspoon *mirin*
1 tablespoon olive oil
1 Sesame Omelet (page 52)
1 spring onion, thinly sliced
$1/2$ green bell pepper, very thinly sliced

1 Slice the mushrooms across, very finely.
2 Combine the soy sauce, sesame oil, lemon juice and *mirin*, and set aside.
3 Heat the olive oil in a small skillet and sauté the mushrooms until soft, about 2 minutes. Remove from the heat and pour the soy mixture over the mushrooms. Stir well and allow to cool completely.
4 Place the Sesame Omelet on a flat work surface, with the seeds facing down. Place the cooled mushroom mixture across the center of the omelet. Sprinkle with the spring onion and bell pepper.
5 Roll the omelet over the filling, to form a cylinder with the filling in the middle.
6 Slice the omelet into quarters at an angle to serve as appetizers, or slice into 10 to 12 smaller rounds for hors d'oeuvres as shown.

Makes 4 large or 10–12 small rolls
Preparation time: **5 mins**
Cooking time: **10 mins**
Assembling time: **10 mins**

Inside-out California Rolls

1 red bell pepper
1 small zucchini, cut lengthwise into 8 strips
1 small, slender Japanese eggplant, halved lengthwise and cut into 2-cm ($3/4$-in) slices
Olive oil for brushing
$1/4$ teaspoon salt
$1/4$ teaspoon freshly ground black pepper
2 sheets *nori*, toasted (page 42) and halved
450 g (3 cups) cooked Sushi Rice (pages 8–9)
60 g ($1/2$ cup) black sesame seeds
150 g (5 oz) mushrooms, sliced and sautéed in olive oil
2 tablespoons Coriander Pesto (page 10)

1 Preheat oven to 180°C (350°F/Gas mark 4). Bake the bell pepper for 20 minutes or until the skin wrinkles. Place under cold, running water to cool and peel the skin off. Deseed and cut it into 1-cm ($1/2$-in) strips.
2 Brush the olive oil over the zucchini and eggplant. Season with the salt and pepper, and bake in the oven until soft, about 5 minutes. Set aside to cool.
3 Cover a sushi mat with a sheet of plastic wrap. Place a half sheet of the *nori* on the mat. Spread $1/3$ of the Sushi Rice evenly over it. Sprinkle with some black sesame seeds and cover with another layer of plastic wrap.
4 Slide one hand under the bottom plastic sheet. Place the other hand over the top plastic sheet. Turn the *nori* and Sushi Rice over so that the sesame seeds are on the bottom and the *nori* is on top. Then, remove the top plastic wrap from the *nori*.
5 Layer the vegetables along the center of the *nori*. Spoon a thin line of the Coriander Pesto close to the bell pepper.
6 Lift the front of the mat together with the sheet of plastic wrap and roll up the sushi. When the front of the mat is 2 cm ($3/4$ in) from the end of the sushi, lift the mat and plastic wrap away from the sushi. Continue rolling to complete the sushi roll.
7 Cut each roll into 8 uniform slices and serve.

Makes 24 slices
Cooking time: **20 mins**
Assembling time: **15 mins**

Inside-out Salmon Sushi Rolls

2 sheets nori, toasted (page 42)
9 thin slices smoked salmon (about 50 g/1 1/2 oz)
450 g (3 cups) cooked Sushi Rice (pages 8–9)
2 tablespoons toasted sesame seeds
1 Japanese cucumber, thinly sliced
3 tablespoons Pickled Ginger (page 18)

1 Using scissors, cut the *nori* into very thin, long strips.
2 Cover a bamboo mat with a sheet of plastic wrap. Place 3 pieces of the smoked salmon on the mat, then spread 1 cup of the Sushi Rice evenly over it. Sprinkle with the toasted sesame seeds.
3 Cover the rice with a second sheet of plastic wrap. Slide one hand under the bottom plastic sheet and place the other hand over the top plastic sheet. Turn the salmon and Sushi Rice sheet over so that the rice covered with sesame seeds is underneath, facing the mat. Remove the plastic wrap from the salmon.
4 Layer the prepared *nori*, cucumber and Pickled Ginger down the center of the salmon.
5 Lift the front of the mat together with the plastic wrap and roll up the sushi, applying even pressure. When the front of the mat is 2 cm (3/4 in) from the end of the sushi, lift the mat and plastic wrap away from the sushi. Continue rolling to complete the sushi roll.
6 Cut each roll into 8 equal slices and serve with soy sauce.

Makes 24 slices
Assembling time: **10 mins**

Salmon Sushi Rolls with Mayonnaise and Fish Roe

10 thin slices smoked salmon, about 60 g (2 oz)
300 g (2 cups) cooked Sushi Rice (pages 8–9)
3 tablespoons Homemade Japanese Mayonnaise (page 11)
1 teaspoon wasabi paste
2 tablespoons flying fish roe or caviar
2 tablespoons chives, thinly sliced

1 Cover a bamboo mat with plastic wrap. Place 5 pieces of the smoked salmon on the mat and spread half of the Sushi Rice on top. Dab half of the wasabi along the center of the rice.
2 Lift the front of the mat and roll the sushi, applying even pressure. When the front of the mat is 2 cm ($^3/_4$ in) from the end of the sushi, pull the mat and plastic wrap away from the sushi. Continue rolling the sushi. The salmon should make a spiral effect through the rice.
3 Cut each roll into 8 uniform slices. Spoon $^1/_2$ teaspoon of the mayonnaise on top of each slice and garnish with the fish roe and chives.

Makes 16 slices
Preparation time: **10 mins**

Index

Ingredients and dips
Abura-age 3
Anago 5
Coriander Pesto 10
Daikon 3
Dashi 3
Dried bonito flakes 3
Fish sauce 3
Furikake 3
Homemade Japanese
  Mayonnaise 11
Kanpyo 4
Katsuo bushi 3
Konbu 4
Lotus root 4
Mirin 4
Miso 4
Nori 4
Palm sugar 4
Pickled Chinese olives 4
Pickled ginger 4
Ponzu 4
Ponzu Sauce 11
Rice vinegar 5
Sake 5
Seasoned jellyfish 5
Sesame oil 5
Sesame paste 5
Sesame Seed Sauce 11
Shiso leaves 5
Shoyu 5
Soy Dipping Sauce 10
Sushi Rice 8
Tezu 5
Wakame 5
Wasabi 5

Battleship Gunkan Sushi
Battleship Gunkan
  Sushi 39
Chicken Teriyaki
  Battleship Sushi 40
Red Salmon Battleship
  Sushi 41

California Rolls
California Rolls 35
Lobster and Mango
  California Rolls 37
Ocean Trout California
  Rolls 36
Thai Prawn California
  Rolls 36

Chirashi Scattered Sushi
Mixed Vegetables on Sushi
  Rice 48

Egg-wrapped Sushi
Egg-wrapped Sushi with
  Mushrooms 54
Sesame Spinach Sushi 50
Sesame Omelet 52
Sesame Omelet with
  Prawns 52
Shiitake Mushroom
  Rolls 57

Hand-formed Nigiri Sushi
Nigiri Sushi with Egg 24
Nigiri Sushi with Prawns,
  Tuna and Eel 22

Hand-rolled Temaki Sushi
Hand-rolled Cone Temaki
  Sushi 42
Temaki Sushi with Asparagus and Smoked Trout 47
Temaki Sushi with Garlic
  Ginger Chicken 44

Inari Tofu Pouch Sushi
Crab Salad Tofu Pouch 29
Inari Tofu Pouch
  Sushi 26

Inside-out Sushi Rolls
Inside–out California
  Rolls 58
Inside-out Salmon Sushi
  Rolls 61
Salmon Sushi Rolls with
  Mayonnaise and Fish
  Roe 62

Maki Sushi Rolls
Cucumber, Crab and
  Salmon Sushi Rolls 30
Smoked Eel and Avocado
  Sushi Rolls 32

Sashimi
Simple Tuna Sashimi 18
Squid with Nori 20
Traditional Seafood Sashimi
  Platter 16
Tuna with Daikon 20

Soups
Flavorful Clear Soup with
  Prawns 14
Healthy Miso Soup with
  Daikon 12
Miso Soup with Tofu and
  Mushrooms 15